What Is the Story of Anne of Green Gables?

by Ellen Labrecque

illustrated by Laurie A. Conley

Penguin Workshop

To Jeff, Sam, and Juliet—Thank you for exploring
Prince Edward Island with me—EL

With love for my mother, who introduced me to
Anne Shirley—LAC

PENGUIN WORKSHOP
An imprint of Penguin Random House LLC, New York

First published in the United States of America by Penguin Workshop,
an imprint of Penguin Random House LLC, New York, 2023

Visit us online at penguinrandomhouse.com.

Library of Congress Cataloging-in-Publication Data is available.

Printed in the United States of America

ISBN 9780593382523 (paperback)   10 9 8 7 6 5 4 3 2 WOR
ISBN 9780593382530 (library binding)   10 9 8 7 6 5 4 3 2 1 WOR

Contents

What Is the Story of Anne of Green Gables?

In the summer of 2008, thousands of people arrived on Prince Edward Island, Canada, to attend an event called "Anne 2008"—a celebration of the one hundredth birthday of the island's most famous fictional resident. Many of the visitors wore straw hats with long, red pigtails attached.

The birthday celebration was in honor of Anne Shirley, the "Anne" in the title of author L. M. Montgomery's 1908 book *Anne of Green Gables*.

Anne Shirley is a smart and funny eleven-year-old girl with red hair and freckles. She goes on many adventures but is also happy getting cozy under a blanket with a good book. Anne is strong-willed and independent. We might say she shows the true spirit of "girl power" today. And she is loyal: Once she is your friend, Anne is your friend for life.

And yet, she has been around for more than 115 years. Anne has many fans and gains new ones every year. When the book starring the character of Anne Shirley turned one hundred, Prince Edward Island planned many events for those fans, including parties, horse-drawn carriage rides, and special readings of *Anne of Green Gables*. Across the island, tourists took photographs in front of Anne statues. They visited gift shops filled with souvenirs including Anne T-shirts, mugs, calendars, magnets, dolls, and, of course, books. Musical performances about *Anne of Green Gables* were performed every day. The farmhouse, named Green Gables, that inspired Anne's fictional home welcomed a steady stream of visitors.

Even though "Anne 2008" is over, thousands
of tourists continue to visit Green Gables every
year. They proudly wear their straw hats to show
that they are, indeed, Anne's friends for life.

CHAPTER 1
Getting to Know Maud

Lucy Maud Montgomery was born on November 30, 1874, in the town of Clifton on Prince Edward Island, Canada, about 250 miles northeast of Canada's border with Maine. She grew up to be called by her middle name, Maud. Her family lived in a small cottage. Her mother, Clara, and father, Hugh, ran a country store that was attached to their home. Soon after Maud was born, her mother became ill with tuberculosis. Tuberculosis (TB) is a lung disease that makes

Lucy Maud Montgomery

it hard for a person to breathe. Today, many countries have a vaccine that prevents TB. But when Maud's mother got sick, it was very deadly. Clara was only twenty-three years old when she died in 1876. Little Maud was just shy of her second birthday.

Maud's father was saddened by his wife's death. He needed to work and didn't think he could raise a child on his own. He took Maud to live with Clara's parents, Lucy and Alexander Macneill.

They had agreed to raise their granddaughter. Lucy and Alexander's home was about seven miles from Clifton. Their farm was located just outside Cavendish—a seaside town on the northern shore of Prince Edward Island.

Maud's grandparents owned one of the nicest homes in Cavendish. It was surrounded by cherry and apple orchards. The house also served as the local post office. It was an important place on the island. Hugh left his daughter with her grandparents and went to find work in Western Canada—far away from Prince Edward Island.

Maud's grandparents were in their fifties.
They had already raised six children of their own.
They hadn't expected to raise another. They fed
their granddaughter hearty meals and gave her a
bedroom in their farmhouse. But they were very
serious people. They did not show Maud much
love and affection.

Prince Edward Island

Prince Edward Island (PEI) is the smallest Canadian province. It is only 174 miles long and forty miles across at its widest point. PEI is in the Gulf of Saint Lawrence, near the Atlantic Ocean. Before 1997, PEI could not be reached by car. But that year, Canada completed the eight-mile-long

Confederation Bridge connecting the island with New Brunswick, on the mainland of Canada.

Only 164,000 people live on Prince Edward Island. They mostly speak English, but some speak French, too.

About 40 percent of PEI is farmland. The island is nicknamed "Spud Island" because it produces the most potatoes of any Canadian province. But PEI is famous for seafood, too, especially mussels and lobster. Every fall the island has the Prince Edward Island International Shellfish Festival celebration.

Prince Edward Island is named after Prince Edward Augustus, the fourth son of King George III, who was king of Great Britain and Ireland from 1760 to 1820. Prince Edward was commander in chief of British North America when the island was named in his honor in 1799.

Even though her grandparents were strict, Maud grew into a lively and imaginative child. She had two make-believe best friends that lived in a cabinet with glass doors. One was named Katie Maurice, and the other was named Lucy Gray.

As a child, Maud spent much of her days outside. She loved to name the plants and trees; she called them Little Syrup, Spotty, Spider, and White Lady Birch.

When Maud was six, she went to school for the first time. The schoolhouse only had one room, and children of all different ages shared the same classroom. When Maud started school, she could already read. With the help of her grandmother, she had been learning since the age of three. Maud loved stories and books. When she wasn't outside playing, she was inside reading. Her grandparents had a well-stocked bookcase filled with leather-bound novels. One of Maud's eventual favorites was *Little Women* by Louisa May Alcott. The story follows the lives of four sisters from childhood into adulthood.

When Maud was seven, two brothers named David and Wellington "Well" Nelson came to live with her and her grandparents. During this time, it was common for friends and neighbors to take in children who needed a home. PEI was a small community, and everybody looked out for one another. The boys' parents had died. And Maud's grandparents had enough space, food, and money to care for them. The boys attended school with Maud and helped out with chores on the farm. Maud and the Nelson brothers became the best of friends. They built playhouses in the orchard and spent hours on the beaches—running in and out of the water.

David and Well stayed with Maud's family for four years. Then they moved to a new home. The years spent living and playing with David and Well Nelson were the happiest of Maud's early life.

CHAPTER 2
A Born Writer

Maud loved to write from an early age. By age nine, she kept a daily diary. She noted the weather and recorded events of her life. She also wrote poems and short stories.

Maud's grandmother and grandfather sent her to bed at 8:00 p.m. every night throughout her childhood. Maud didn't mind. She devoted time

to writing before going to sleep. As she sat at her
desk, she looked out her window at the family
orchard and the distant sea.

In the summer of 1890, when Maud was fifteen, she left Prince Edward Island and traveled by train to live with her father, who was now living in the town of Prince Albert in the Saskatchewan

province of Canada, thousands of miles from PEI.

Maud was thrilled to reunite with her father. "Oh, it was delightful to see dear father again," Maud wrote.

Oh, Canada

Canada is the second-largest country in the world after Russia. It spans over 3,400 miles from east to west and more than 2,800 miles from north to south! It is made up of ten provinces and three territories.

More than 40 percent of Canada's land is in the Arctic Circle, where it is freezing cold and not easy to live. Canada has a population of only thirty-seven million people. (The United States' population, by comparison, is over 330 million.) Over 90 percent of Canadians live within one hundred miles of the United States' border.

Today Canada's population is made up of many different cultures including people of English, Scottish, French, First Nations, Inuit, and Métis heritage.

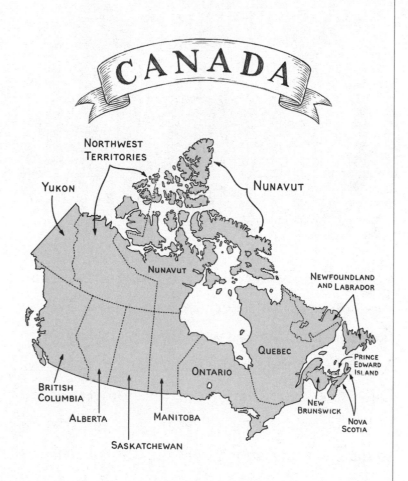

CANADA

NORTHWEST
TERRITORIES

YUKON

NUNAVUT

NUNAVUT

NEWFOUNDLAND
AND LABRADOR

QUEBEC

ONTARIO

PRINCE
EDWARD
ISLAND

BRITISH
COLUMBIA

NEW
BRUNSWICK

NOVA
SCOTIA

ALBERTA

MANITOBA

SASKATCHEWAN

But this feeling didn't last long, and Maud
was homesick for Prince Edward Island. Maud's
father had remarried a woman named Mary Anne
McRae, and they had a baby daughter, Maud's
half-sister, Kate. Mary Anne did not treat Maud
well. She was jealous of Maud and didn't want
to share her husband's attention. She told Maud's
father that he must stop calling his daughter
"Maudie," his nickname for her.

In February 1891, Maud's father and stepmother had another baby, a son named Donald. Maud was asked to stay home from school to help with housework and to take care of the baby. Now that Maud was home all the time, Mary Anne spent even more time being unkind to her stepdaughter. Maud would have

preferred to be back in school. She began having constant headaches and longed to go back to her grandparents. Maud returned to Prince Edward Island in the summer of 1891.

Maud finished high school when she was sixteen. During this time, most women married young—even as early as Maud's age. Many did not even finish high school. But Maud wasn't like other young women. She wasn't ready to be married. After high school, she went to Prince of Wales College in Charlottetown, the capital of

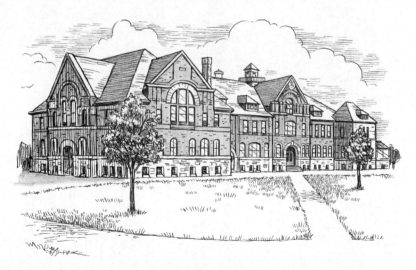

Prince of Wales College

PEI, to study to become a teacher. She worked hard and took two years' worth of classes in one year. This was enough to earn her teacher's certificate.

Over the next several years, Maud taught at small schools on Prince Edward Island. For a brief time, she also worked as a copy editor at a newspaper in Halifax—the largest city in the

nearby province of Nova Scotia. No matter what job Maud had, she always found time to write. Many of her short stories and poems were published in magazines and newspapers across Canada and the United States.

A poem about apple picking was published in a Philadelphia magazine called *Golden Days*. Another, "Fisher Lassies," was published in a well-known magazine called *The Youth's Companion*. Many of Maud's poems were about nature. They described the natural beauty of Prince Edward Island. Her short stories usually had a moral—they were supposed to teach children and adults how to behave in the world. Maud later admitted she didn't especially like writing these kinds of stories, but they were what magazines wanted to publish at the time. Instead, Maud really wanted to write stories that were "fun for fun's sake."

In 1898, when Maud was twenty-three, her grandfather, Alexander Macneill, died. Maud moved back into her childhood home, the old farmhouse, to keep her grandmother company. In 1903, a Canadian newspaper published an article about Prince Edward Island poets. Maud, now twenty-nine, was mentioned as one of the best writers on the island!

CHAPTER 3
Anne Arrives

In the spring of 1905, Maud, now age thirty, came across a note in her journal that would change her life. It was a summary of a newspaper story that she had once read. The note said,

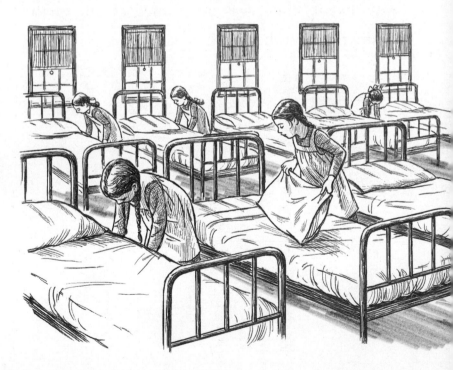

"Elderly couple apply to orphan asylum for a boy. By mistake a girl is sent."

An orphanage, or orphan asylum as the newspaper stated, is a group home where children live while waiting to be adopted by another family. Orphaned children are those who have lost both of their parents. In the twenty-first century, children live with temporary families—called foster homes—while they wait to be adopted into a permanent home.

In Maud's time, orphaned children were sent
to homes without even meeting their new families!
It was much harder to travel and for people to
get to know one another first. The children being
adopted usually became farmworkers and helpers
in their new households. And there were plenty

of orphaned children who needed homes! It was much more common for adults to die at younger ages than it is today.

Based on the note in her journal, Maud began writing the outline for a new book. Maud wanted this story to be different from what she had written for the magazines. She decided to write about a not-so-perfect but very lovable girl. Maud named her Anne Shirley.

Maud's story began by describing an adult brother and sister, Matthew and Marilla Cuthbert, who live together in a home they called Green Gables. Maud made up a name for their town, Avonlea, which just happened to be on Prince Edward Island. The story was set in the 1870s.

Because Matthew Cuthbert needs help taking care of Green Gables—doing chores such as chopping wood and feeding their horses—he and his sister decide to adopt a boy from an orphanage in Nova Scotia. When Matthew rides to the train station, he discovers that a girl named Anne has arrived instead. Anne is a slender eleven-year-old girl with bright red hair.

Matthew wants to send Anne back to Nova Scotia. He doesn't believe she can help him with all the farmwork. But Anne is desperate for a family of her own. She begs Matthew to let her stay. And so he agrees to at least bring Anne back to Green Gables to see what Marilla thinks about their unexpected guest.

Anne is a happy and talkative child. Matthew, who is shy, likes Anne right away.

On the horse-drawn carriage ride back to Green Gables, Anne does most of the talking while Matthew listens. One thing she tells Matthew is how much she dislikes her red hair.

"I can't be perfectly happy," Anne says. "Nobody could who has red hair. It will be my lifelong sorrow."

The Gift of Gab

Anne Shirley likes to talk *a lot*. She uses very descriptive language to express her grand ideas. Anne's colorful way of speaking is one of the reasons fans are so devoted to her. Many of her well-known sayings are about the importance of good friends, having a positive outlook, and how beautiful nature can be:

"It's been my experience that you can nearly always enjoy things if you make up your mind firmly that you will."

"Look at that sea, girls—all silver and shadow and vision of things not seen. We couldn't enjoy its loveliness anymore if we had millions of dollars and ropes of diamonds."

"True friends are always together in spirit."

"Dear old world, you are very lovely, and I am glad to be alive in you."

At this time, some people actually felt the same way Anne did. They thought that red hair was not very pretty! The fact that Maud Montgomery created Anne's character with red hair was significant. It made her even more of an outsider arriving on Prince Edward Island than she already was.

By the time Anne and Matthew arrive at Green Gables, Matthew already knows he would like Anne to stay. But Anne has to convince Marilla Cuthbert, who isn't as easily charmed as her brother had been. She is a serious woman who doesn't easily warm up to children—especially one who is as outgoing and talkative as Anne. Anne tries her best to convince Marilla that she could be just as useful, or more useful, than any boy: "I'll try to do and be anything you want me, if you'll only keep me."

But Marilla is determined to send Anne back to the orphanage in Nova Scotia.

The next day, during a horse-and-buggy ride, Anne tells Marilla about her early life. Both of Anne's parents died when she was just a baby. Neither of her parents had any living relatives, so a housekeeper named Mrs. Thomas took Anne home to live with her. Anne lived with Mrs. Thomas and her husband until she was eight. But she didn't have an easy life with the Thomases, who sometimes hit her. Anne was then sent to live with another family where she cared for six children—three sets of twins! Finally, Anne went to live in the orphanage. She barely had the chance to go to school. But she made up for her lack of education by reading every chance she could.

Anne's story makes Marilla Cuthbert feel sorry for the young girl. She feels sad that nobody had ever really cared for or loved Anne.

In her heart, Marilla knows she cannot leave Anne to become the servant of another family or return her to the orphanage. Marilla and Anne

return home together. Matthew is so happy to see them both. Marilla has decided to let Anne stay for good. Now, she finally has a home—and her very own bedroom.

Maud describes the scene outside of Anne's bedroom window as having "lush" fields, cherry trees "showered over with blossoms," and grass "sprinkled with dandelions." There is also "a sparkling blue glimpse of sea." Anne's "beauty-loving eyes lingered on it all."

Learning that Matthew and Marilla have agreed to let her stay at Green Gables, Anne says, "I'm glad as glad can be." She continues, "Oh, glad doesn't seem the right word at all. . . . [I]t's something more than glad. I'm so happy. I'll try to be so good!"

CHAPTER 4
Home

Once Anne knows she is staying with Matthew and Marilla, her daily adventures begin.

Anne goes to school in a one-room schoolhouse, just like Maud did as a child.

In school, Anne strives for the highest grades and honors in the class. She is a girl who goes after what she wants.

"It's delightful to have ambitions," she concludes at one point. "I'm so glad I have such a lot."

Diana Barry

Anne's best friend is a pretty yet shy girl named Diana Barry. Anne feels that she can "confide my inmost soul" to Diana.

Gilbert Blythe

Anne also meets Gilbert Blythe, the smartest and most popular boy in school. He likes Anne right away. He admires how smart, ambitious, and brave she is. And he notices how different she is from the other girls. But Gilbert doesn't know how to express his feelings. Instead, he gets Anne's attention by teasing her.

Anne of Green Gables takes place over five years—from the time Anne is eleven years old until she is sixteen. It is a story of a girl's search for her place in the world and the family she creates along the way. Her journey is about the importance of being herself. Anne asks the world to accept her for who she is, not for who people expect her to be.

Many of the chapters in the book take place in June—Maud Montgomery's favorite month. At first, small events in Anne's life take up entire chapters, such as a Sunday church picnic or a day in school when Gilbert pulls Anne's braids and makes fun of her red hair by calling out "Carrots! Carrots!" Because Anne is so sensitive about her red hair, this makes her furious. She breaks a

chalk slate over Gilbert's head and exclaims, "You mean, hateful boy! How dare you!"

She gets in trouble for this violent outburst, and the teacher makes her write on the chalkboard:

"Ann Shirley has a very bad temper." She is forced to stand at the board under these words for the rest of the afternoon.

The name *Ann* printed on the board makes Anne especially mad because she likes to spell her name with an *e* on the end of it. She added the *e* because she thinks it makes her more special and different. "A-n-n looks dreadful," she says, "but A-n-n-e looks so much more distinguished."

After the fight, Anne remains proud of herself for standing up to Gilbert and vows never to speak or look at him again. But Gilbert secretly admires Anne's willfulness and courage.

Anne gets into other kinds of trouble outside
of school as well. By accident, she dyes her hair
green. And she once gave her best friend, Diana,

wine to drink! But as Anne grows up, the chapters of each book begin to cover years of her life instead of just a single day. After Anne finishes her education at the one-room schoolhouse, she heads to Queen's Academy in Charlottetown to study for her teaching degree. She then wins a scholarship to Redmond College in Kingsport, Nova Scotia. Anne planned on spending four years at college earning her degree, but Matthew suddenly dies of a heart attack and Marilla begins to go blind. Anne decides to stay at Green Gables and help Marilla instead of going to Kingsport for college.

She hopes to teach at the Avonlea school, the same school where she had been a student. Unfortunately, the school has already hired a new teacher: Gilbert Blythe! But once he discovers that Anne gave up her dream of going to college to stay home and help Marilla, Gilbert lets Anne have the job. He then takes a teaching job in another town.

When Anne learns that Gilbert did this for her, she forgives him for all of his childhood teasing. She and Gilbert finally become friends. "We are going to be the best of friends," Gilbert says to Anne after she forgives him. "You've thwarted destiny long enough."

The last chapter of the book is titled "The Bend in the Road," hinting that Anne's life is now heading into adulthood. Anne is very happy with her place in the world and content to remain at Green Gables and teach at the local school—at least for now.

After rooting for the headstrong girl to attain her dreams, readers realized they loved Anne just as much when she postponed her goals in order to take care of her family. Although this could seem like a disappointing ending, it makes the character of Anne feel very real. Sometimes life's responsibilities can get in the way of dreams.

In the last line of the novel, Anne whispers:

". . . all's right with the world."

CHAPTER 5
An Instant Sensation

Good advice for any writer is often, "Write what you know." Maud Montgomery took that lesson to heart. There is no denying that Anne and Maud shared similarities. Anne has an imaginary best friend named Katie Maurice, just like Maud did as a child. Many of the people Maud knew growing up were inspirations for some of Anne's friends and neighbors. Marilla Cuthbert is a lot like Maud's own grandmother. She is strict but grows to love Anne as a daughter.

The Prince Edward Island setting was certainly borrowed from Maud's own life. Green Gables was based on a relative's farmhouse, not too far from Maud's grandparents' home. Avonlea was based on Cavendish, the real-life small town where Maud lived.

Lover's Lane

The natural setting of the island is also an important part of the book. The novel is filled with detailed descriptions of flowers, the woods, the sea, and the sunsets and sunrises. Just as Maud did as a child, Anne gives special names to plants, trees, and places close to her home. Most famously, she calls a path in the woods "Lover's Lane," and another section of the forest is the "Haunted Wood."

Because their lives were so similar, it's not surprising that Maud wrote in her journal that "*Anne* is as real to me as if I had given her birth: as real and as dear." She had begun the novel in the spring of 1905 and wrote for about three hours a day until it was finished in the following year.

Once Maud finished, she typed up the entire manuscript on an old typewriter with a broken *w* key. She went back and filled in every *w* on each page by hand.

In early 1906, the manuscript was finished. Maud sent it to five different publishers in Indianapolis, New York, and Boston. When one publisher rejected it, she would mail it right back out to another. The mail took a long time to reach Prince Edward Island, but Maud checked her mailbox regularly, hopeful to hear some good news. But each publisher had rejected her story.

Feeling defeated, Maud gave up and put the manuscript in a hatbox. She continued to work on other stories and poems. Maud rediscovered the novel a year later when she was doing some spring cleaning. She decided to send it out once again. This time, she sent it to L. C. Page & Company, Inc., a publisher in Boston, Massachusetts. On April 15, 1907, Maud received a letter: L. C. Page & Company, Inc., wanted to publish *Anne of Green Gables.*

The publisher, Louis Coues Page, gave Maud a choice: She could accept a one-time payment of $500 for her book. Or she could agree to a royalty contract. In this agreement, Maud would receive 10 percent of the price of every book that was sold (about nine cents for each one.)

Louis Coues Page

Many, many copies of *Anne of Green Gables* would have to be sold in order for Maud to earn more than the $500 Mr. Page was offering her.

But Maud decided to choose the royalty payment agreement, anyway. She knew it was a risky choice, but she believed in her book. She wanted to take the chance on herself and on Anne.

The decision was one of the smartest of her life. She also insisted that her name on the book be written as L. M. Montgomery, the same name she had previously published her stories and poetry with.

In June 1908, *Anne of Green Gables* was finally published. It became popular right away. Major newspapers all over Canada and the United States wrote positive reviews. One said that "the book radiates happiness and optimism." Another newspaper writer said, "*Anne of Green Gables* . . . has made an instantaneous hit. . . . Beyond doubt, *Anne of Green Gables* is well worth reading."

Maud published her book at the perfect time. The literacy rate—a measure of the amount of people who can read—was steadily rising across the world at the beginning of the twentieth century. This meant there were more people who wanted to read good stories with memorable characters. It wasn't just children who were reading the Anne novel—people of all ages loved it.

The book sold nineteen thousand copies in the first five months. Maud received her first royalty payment of $1,730. This was more than triple the amount she would have earned if she had taken the one-time payment! And there would be many more royalty payments to come.

"Not bad for the first six months of a new book by an unknown author," Maud said.

CHAPTER 6
Fans from Everywhere

Fan letters from readers of *Anne of Green Gables* began arriving for Maud—hundreds of them! Maud made sure to respond to each one. The letters weren't just sent from the local Prince Edward Island area—they arrived from all over the world. One day she received eighty-five letters from Australia alone!

Some readers believed that Maud Montgomery was a long-lost relative. They wanted to connect with the author as if she were a part of their own families. But because the book listed only her initials, L. M., they did not know if she was man or a woman. One letter to Maud began, "My dear long-lost uncle." And many of the letters were even addressed to Anne Shirley, as if she was a real person.

Other fans of the book wanted to know where Maud came up with her ideas. They asked if she was a lot like Anne in real life. They were curious if the other characters in the books were based on real people, too. But most of all, they wanted Maud to write many more books about Anne so that they could learn how the rest of her life turns out. And they especially wanted to tell Maud how much they enjoyed reading her novel.

One fan letter that made Maud especially happy and proud was from the famous American author Mark Twain.

Mark Twain

"Anne of Green Gables is the dearest and most moving and delightful child since the immortal Alice [in Wonderland]," Twain wrote, referring to the beloved character that had been created by Lewis Carroll over forty years earlier.

Mark Twain (1835–1910)

Mark Twain is the pen name of a man who was born Samuel Langhorne Clemens in Florida, Missouri, near the banks of the Mississippi River. In his youth, he spent a lot of time on the water and dreamed of one day being a steamboat pilot.

Instead, he became a famous writer. Mark Twain is one of America's most beloved authors and humorists. He is best known for his two young adult books *The Adventures of Tom Sawyer* and *The Adventures of Huckleberry Finn.* Both novels,

which touch on serious themes like racism and social injustice, tell the stories of two young boys rafting on the Mississippi River and the people and places they encounter. He wrote *The Adventures of Tom Sawyer* in 1876 and followed up with its sequel, *The Adventures of Huckleberry Finn*, nine years later.

Twain wrote many other adventurous stories and comical tales. He was also famous for funny and clever quotations, including "Always obey your parents, when they are present."

CHAPTER 7
Her Story Continues

Maud began writing the sequel, her next book to continue the story of *Anne of Green Gables*, almost immediately. Within a year, she published

her second Anne book— *Anne of Avonlea.* The title of the novel lets the reader know how Anne's world is growing. She is no longer just *Anne of Green Gables* but now Anne of the village.

The sequel was published in 1909 with almost as much success as the first book. It tells the story of the two years of Anne's life from age sixteen to eighteen, when she is a teacher in Avonlea. Anne is still full of imagination and charm. And she still gets herself into funny situations. In one scene, she accidently dabs red dye on her nose before meeting a famous author. (She thought she was using a lotion to rub off her freckles but instead used some of Marilla's red dye.)

"First I dye my hair; then I dye my nose. Marilla cut my hair off when I dyed it but that remedy would hardly be practicable in this case," Anne says. She was hoping no one would cut off her nose!

Mrs. Lynde

By the end of the second novel, the Cuthberts' neighbor, Mrs. Lynde, moves in with Marilla and Anne. Because of Marilla's continuing problems with her sight, Mrs. Lynde helps out around the house. This allows Anne to "dust" her ambitions and finally head to Redmond College in Kingsport. Gilbert Blythe, who is now a good friend of Anne's, leaves for college as well. Readers were excited to imagine that Anne and Gilbert might one day become a couple.

"Perhaps, after all, romance did not come into one's life with pomp and blare; . . . perhaps it crept to one's side like an old friend through quiet ways," Anne said.

The Order of the Anne Books

There are eight books in the Anne of Green Gables series. The first three, *Anne of Green Gables*, *Anne of Avonlea*, and *Anne of the Island* were published in order between 1908 and 1915. Maud then published three more over the next six years: *Anne's House of Dreams*, *Rainbow Valley*, and *Rilla of Ingleside*.

But years later, in the 1930s, Maud published two more books that are set earlier than *Rainbow*

Valley and *Rilla of Ingleside.* These novels fill in the stories of Anne's life that were not included in the first six books. By this time, Maud Montgomery had moved on to writing other books and stories about different characters. So why go back to Anne?

"It was like going home," Maud explained.

"She is so real," Maud had written about Anne, "I shall lift my eyes . . . and find her by my side."

Here is the order of Anne books according to Anne's age, along with the date each was published.

1. *Anne of Green Gables* (1908)

2. *Anne of Avonlea* (1909)

3. *Anne of the Island* (1915)

4. *Anne of Windy Poplars* (1936)

5. *Anne's House of Dreams* (1917)

6. *Anne of Ingleside* (1939)

7. *Rainbow Valley* (1919)

8. *Rilla of Ingleside* (1921)

Over the next eleven years, Maud wrote and published four more Anne Shirley novels (the final two would come years later).

The third book in the series, *Anne of the Island*, follows Anne during her four years at Redmond College. It ends with a marriage proposal from Gilbert—which Anne accepts. Anne calls the day Gilbert proposes "the birthday" of their happiness.

Marriage was very much on Maud's mind at this time of her life. She herself had gotten married in between publishing *Anne of Avonlea* and *Anne of the Island*. She married Reverend Ewan Macdonald on July 5, 1911, when she was thirty-six years old. After a honeymoon in Scotland and England, the couple moved to the small town of Leaskdale near Toronto, Ontario, Canada. Reverend Macdonald was the leader of a church there, and Maud continued to write. Thanks to Anne, Maud was quite popular. On

Sundays, people packed into her husband's church for services. Although they were there for worship, they also wanted to see L. M. Montgomery, the reverend's famous wife.

Maud and Ewan

Maud's fourth book of the series, *Anne of Windy Poplars*, takes place over three years. In this book, Gilbert is in medical school and Anne works as the principal of a school on Prince Edward Island. She and Gilbert write letters to each other and see each other on holidays back in Avonlea. In the fifth book, *Anne's House of Dreams*, Anne and Gilbert, now a doctor, marry and live in a house in the seaside town of Four Winds on

Prince Edward Island. Their home is on property that has many trees and a brook that runs right through the center.

She and Gilbert have their first child, a daughter named Joy, who dies soon after birth. But by the end of the book, Anne gives birth to a healthy son, James Matthew. Anne and Gilbert and their new baby move to a bigger home, which they name Ingleside. The house is closer to town, making it easier for Gilbert to work as a doctor. Anne says she will always consider their first home by the sea the "house of her dreams."

Maud and her husband had two boys themselves—Chester Cameron, born in 1912, and Ewan Stuart, born in 1915. In between the boys' births, Maud also lost a baby soon after he was born, just like her character Anne had.

Maud's days were busy. She wrote in two-hour shifts every morning. The rest of the day she spent taking care of her two young sons and the family home.

At this time, Maud was also having difficulties with her publisher, L. C. Page & Company, Inc. Mr. Page had been reprinting Maud's books but not paying her royalty payments for the new sales. In 1919, Maud traveled to Boston to challenge Mr. Page in court. She won the court case and was paid the money that L. C. Page & Company, Inc., owed her. But Maud also made a deal with Mr. Page to sell him all the rights to the books she had already published. He paid her a total sum of $20,000. Although this seemed like a lot of money at the time, it proved to be an unwise financial decision for Maud. L. C. Page & Company, Inc., would eventually earn a lot more money from selling movie and other rights of all the Anne Shirley stories. Maud signed on with a new Canadian publisher, McClelland, Goodchild & Stewart.

With every passing year, Anne was discovered by newer generations of readers, and Maud became even more famous. In 1923, at age forty-nine, she became the first Canadian woman to be named a member of the British Royal Society of Arts and Letters. This was a huge honor for an author. Four years later, the prime minister of England, Stanley Baldwin, wrote a fan letter to Maud and even wanted to pay her a visit.

Stanley Baldwin

The First Anne Movie

The very first *Anne of Green Gables* movie was made in 1919. It was a silent film produced in Hollywood. It was the very first movie role for actress Mary Miles Minter, who played Anne and went on to star in over fifty more silent films.

Because it was an American production, the film's location was Dedham, Massachusetts, instead of Prince Edward Island. When the character of Anne graduates from college, a US flag is seen flying in the background, not a Canadian one.

Maud was upset by all the changes that had been made to her original Anne story. She later wrote in her diary, "I think if I hadn't already known it was from my book, that I would never have recognized it."

The second *Anne of Green Gables* movie—this time with dialogue—arrived fifteen years later, in 1934. Anne was played by a young actress who changed her real name to . . . Anne Shirley!

"It would give me keen pleasure to have an opportunity of shaking your hand and thanking you for the pleasure your books have given me," the prime minister wrote.

Although Maud never did get to meet Prime Minister Baldwin, she wrote in her journal how happy she was that he was a fan.

"[I] read [his letter] not to myself but to the little girl who wrote her dreams into books that have pleased a statesman of the Empire."

CHAPTER 8
Worldwide Fame

Anne of Ingleside is the sixth book in the series, but it was the last to be written. Published in 1939, it is set in the fictional seaside village of Ingleside on Prince Edward Island, and it updates the story of Anne and Gilbert, along with the adventures of their six children. The story is set in the years

around 1900, before the events she described in *Rainbow Valley* and *Rilla of Ingleside*, two books she'd published almost twenty years earlier.

By 1939, the world had changed quite a bit since Anne had first been introduced over thirty years earlier. World War I had been fought, and a Great Depression had ruined businesses and economic stability around the world. And some of the same rival European countries that had fought World War I were in the middle of another battle that would eventually become World War II. Maybe because of all the uncertainty and upheaval, Anne was as popular as ever.

Readers looked to the Anne Shirley stories to escape their own troubles and spend time in the simpler and happier days of Anne's life. The Polish army gave copies of *Anne of Green Gables*, or *Ania z Zielonego Wzgórza*, as it was called in Polish, to their soldiers during the war.

The book was intended to remind them what
they were fighting to defend—including values
such as love, home, family, and freedom.

Hiroshima and Nagasaki

By the summer of 1945, Germany had been defeated by the United States and its allies. But Japan, who fought on the same side as Germany in World War II, refused to surrender.

For four years, a group of scientists led by the American physicist J. Robert Oppenheimer had been working to develop an atomic bomb, a powerful new weapon made by splitting an atom of the element uranium. On August 6, 1945, the United States dropped the first-ever atomic bomb on the city of Hiroshima, Japan. The bomb flattened five square miles of the city and killed more than 140,000 people. Three days later, the United States dropped a second atomic bomb on the Japanese city of Nagasaki, killing another 80,000 people. Japan finally surrendered to the Allies.

After the bombings, thousands of Japanese children were left without a mother or a father. They were nicknamed the "A-bomb orphans."

In 1939, a Canadian missionary who was living in Japan left a copy of *Anne of Green Gables* with a friend, Hanako Muraoka, who was a translator. Muraoka read the book, loved it, and then translated it from English into Japanese. She renamed it *Akage no An* (Red-Haired Anne).

Anne's popularity continued to rise, especially in Japan, where more than 120,000 children had become orphaned by the end of the war.

After World War II ended, Anne's cheerful story was the perfect book for many Japanese children who were suffering from the pain and loss of their families as an effect of the war. Anne's story was especially comforting to them. Anne Shirley had lost her parents, too, but she found love and a home at Green Gables with a new kind of family.

Although Anne's story was a happy one, Maud Montgomery wasn't as lucky in her own life. Her husband, Ewan, suffered from depression and eventually could no longer work as a minister. Maud's oldest son, Chester, borrowed money from his mother but never paid it back. His behavior broke Maud's heart.

In 1936, Maud, now sixty-two, and Ewan moved to a house in Toronto called Journey's End. Unfortunately, the house turned out to be perfectly named. Ewan's health continued to decline.

Journey's End

Anne in Japan

In 1952, *Anne of Green Gables* became an official part of Japan's public-school reading curriculum. Soon it seemed like all of Japan had fallen for the red-headed heroine. They admired her hardworking attitude and her ability to bounce back after tragedy. Japanese schools were named in her honor, national Anne fan clubs were organized, and many Japanese brides got married at Anne-themed weddings. Today, there is even a "Canadian World" national park in Japan where a replica of Green Gables and other buildings in Avonlea can be found.

Thousands of Japanese tourists also flock to Prince Edward Island every year to visit the house that inspired Green Gables and the Anne stories.

He was depressed, and Maud grew quite sad as well. She published two more books in the Anne series after she moved to Journey's End. But although she still wrote novels and personal journals, Maud didn't write every day.

"Thank God," Maud had written in her journal at one point, "I can keep the shadows of my life out of my work. I would not wish to darken any other life—I want instead to be a messenger of optimism and sunshine." Maud was careful to continue writing a happy life for her character, but Maud's life no longer matched Anne's.

A thousand miles away, Prince Edward Island continued to celebrate Anne. In 1937, the Canadian government bought the farmhouse that belonged to Maud's relatives—the inspiration for Green Gables—and created a national park. In addition to the farmhouse, the park contained beaches and orchard groves that were all described in the Anne Shirley novels. A house built by her aunt and uncle was also turned into a museum.

On April 24, 1942, at age sixty-seven, Lucy Maud Montgomery died in her sleep. Her funeral took place five days later on Prince Edward Island at the local Cavendish church. The school was closed for the afternoon so that students could attend the funeral. The crowd at the service was so large it couldn't fit inside the church. Maud was buried near the schoolyard she had played in as a child. Her obituary appeared in newspapers around the world. Some newspapers noted that Maud was buried "in a little cemetery near the surf and sand dunes of Prince Edward Island's north shore . . . amid the surroundings she portrayed for millions of young readers."

Maud, like Anne, would forever be a part of Prince Edward Island.

CHAPTER 9
Forever Loved

Anne of Green Gables has been translated into at least thirty-six languages, the most of any book by a Canadian author. More than fifty million copies of the various Anne stories have been sold all over the world. Maud's journals—which she kept her entire life—have also been published.

Maud's youngest son, Dr. E. Stuart Macdonald, saved the diaries his mother wrote from 1889, when she was fifteen, until her death in 1942, when she was sixty-seven. In 1981, he sold them to the University of Guelph in Ontario, Canada.

Selected journals were eventually published by Oxford University Press in five different volumes, beginning in 2000. These journals allowed readers to study Maud's thoughts and the details of her life. When people read Maud's early journals, they often recognize the voice of her most famous character, Anne.

Anne of Green Gables has been made into movies and at least six television miniseries. A 1985 miniseries won an Emmy Award—television's highest honor. Old and new fans

watch *Anne with an "E"* on Netflix, a series that was released in 2017. The title of the show recalls that day when Anne stood at the chalkboard as a punishment, early in the first book.

Additionally, *Anne of Green Gables: The Musical*, produced annually in Charlottetown (not far from Cavendish) since 1965, was named the longest-running annual musical in the world in 2014. It has also been staged in New York,

London, and Japan. There is even a ballet named in Anne's honor.

Tiny PEI welcomes more than a million and a half visitors each year. Most are fans of the books who come to see where Maud grew up and where Anne was created. Some of the visitors are very famous. Prince William and Kate Middleton, Prince and Princess of Wales, visited Prince Edward Island on their first royal trip in 2011. Kate said *Anne of Green Gables* had been her favorite book growing up. Author, director, and actress Mindy Kaling has said, "The . . . book world I would like to live in is *Anne of Green Gables*."

In 2015, a first-edition copy of the 1908 *Anne of Green Gables* book sold for nearly $29,000. That same year, Google created a Google Doodle on November 30—which would have been Maud's 141st birthday. The doodle included drawings of the most memorable scenes from the book.

Anne's story is about an imperfect young girl

Catherine, Princess of Wales, and a fan

who loves life even though she has overcome the loss of her parents and a difficult beginning to her life. Readers want to see Anne succeed. They feel they are on a journey with her as she grows from one stage of her life to the next. Anne's story is about optimism and finally finding the place

you belong. It is also about the hope that all will be well. Maybe not right away or tomorrow, but someday. This is a message that was powerful for readers in 1908 and is still important over a century later.

Bibliography

*Books for young readers

Andronik, Catherine M. *Kindred Spirit: A Biography of L. M. Montgomery, Creator of Anne of Green Gables*. New York: Atheneum, 1993.

Gammel, Irene. *Looking For Anne of Green Gables: The Life and Times of L. M. Montgomery*. New York: St. Martin's Press, 2008.

*Gillen, Mollie. *The Wheel of Things: A Biography of L. M. Montgomery*. Halifax, Canada: Formac Publishing Company, 1975.

*Montgomery, L. M. *The Complete Anne of Green Gables*. London, England: Starfire Publishing, 1998.

Prince Edward Island, Canada. "Anne of Green Gables: All Things Anne." Tourism PEI. https://www.tourismpei.com/anne-of-green-gables.

Rosenberg, Liz. *House of Dreams: The Life of L. M. Montgomery*. Somerville, MA: Candlewick Press, 2018.

Rubio, Mary Henley. *Lucy Maud Montgomery: The Gift of Wings*. Toronto, Canada: Anchor Canada, 2008.

Rubio, Mary, and Elizabeth Waterston, editors. *The Selected Journals of L. M. Montgomery: Volume IV 1929–1935*. Oxford, England: Oxford University Press, 1998.

Rubio, Mary, and Elizabeth Waterson. *Writing a Life: L. M. Montgomery*. Toronto, Canada: ECW Press, 1995.

Timeline of Anne of Green Gables

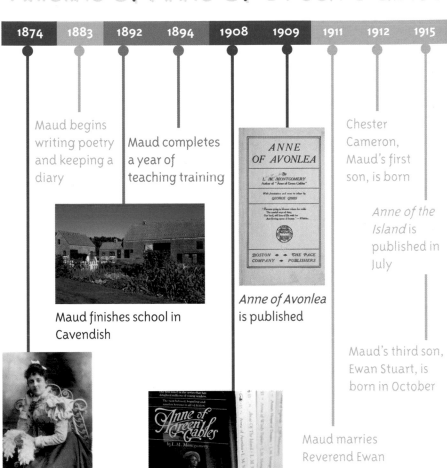

1874 — Lucy Maud Montgomery is born on November 30 in Clifton, Prince Edward Island

1883 — Maud begins writing poetry and keeping a diary

1892 — Maud finishes school in Cavendish

1894 — Maud completes a year of teaching training

1908 — *Anne of Green Gables* is published by L. C. Page & Company, Inc., and sells nineteen thousand copies in its first five months

1909 — *Anne of Avonlea* is published

1911 — Maud marries Reverend Ewan Macdonald in July

1912 — Chester Cameron, Maud's first son, is born

1915 — *Anne of the Island* is published in July; Maud's third son, Ewan Stuart, is born in October

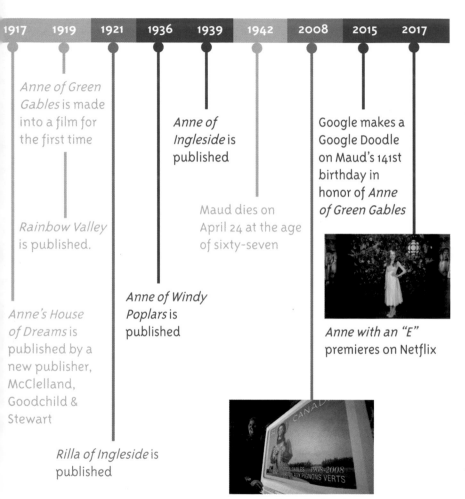

| 1917 | 1919 | 1921 | 1936 | 1939 | 1942 | 2008 | 2015 | 2017 |

Anne of Green Gables is made into a film for the first time

Anne of Ingleside is published

Google makes a Google Doodle on Maud's 141st birthday in honor of *Anne of Green Gables*

Rainbow Valley is published.

Maud dies on April 24 at the age of sixty-seven

Anne with an "E" premieres on Netflix

Anne's House of Dreams is published by a new publisher, McClelland, Goodchild & Stewart

Anne of Windy Poplars is published

Rilla of Ingleside is published

Prince Edward Island celebrates the one hundredth anniversary of the publication of *Anne of Green Gables*